Intequinism

Marquard Dirk Pienaar

MPhil (Philosophy)

Published from Pretoria by *Africahead*

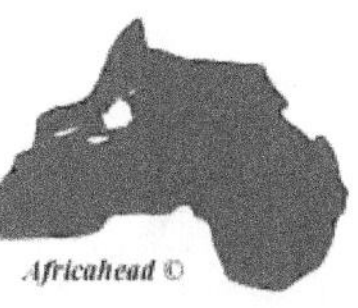

Moiom cc transacting as *Africahead*
Eaton Hall E309
Visagie Street 266
Pretoria
Gauteng
0001
South Africa.

First published digitally during November 2017.
This Amazon paperback version published first during December 2019.
ISBN: 978-0-9946-6312-2.

Critique can be addressed to author by **e-mail**: mdpienaar@africahead.co.za.

Table of Contents

Bertrand Russell was asked what message he wanted to give to future generations. His answer was to respect the ideas Truth and Love. This book rationalises Bertrand Russell's philosophical conclusion. The author does not agree with everything Russell promoted, but with regard to Truth and Love, being the primary principles, above selves, they agree.

Bertrand Russell, giving his message, can be seen at: https://www.youtube.com/watch?v=ihaB8AFOhZo[1].

The whole interview can be seen at: https://www.youtube.com/watch?v=1bZv3pSaLtY[2].

---

[1] Accessed on 15 October 2017
[2] Accessed on 15 October 2017

Introduction

What does the coming "Kingdom of God" imply? Basically it means, nowhere, a government ever existed, which is 'universally' accepted as a just government. If such a government existed it would not have been overthrown.

Although this book contains autobiographical information in "the first person", the purpose is not to give an autobiographical account. The purpose is to motivate a new philosophy called *Intequinism,* and to demonstrate how many people in society, are influenced negatively, like me, because of the way utilitarianism functions, and to motivate, that has a negative influence on society, due to inhibiting good creativity. Aristotle's antiquated conviction that something, which is good for self, cannot be good for another, was also accepted in the sense; what is good for some has to be bad for others. Aristotle's view does not consider, creativities can benefit universally, when development considers realism. By realism I mean, although holistic views are impossible for individuals each, groups can consider enough relevant information to implement new creativities to benefit all. This book demonstrates how the system outlaws and ostracise creative people, and we are then, if we want to continue living, forced to become, for example, outlaws or vagrants. The system then continues to parasitise us by telling our tragic stories in the media, for maximum profit, whilst advertising hope in Christ, who will never come in singular form. The only hope for a Christlike change is for the system to change and for many people to change with it, on the way to better lives for all.

Generally, people will agree that the "Kingdom of God" has not settled on Earth. That means, through all the ages, a dominant paradigm in each age existed, through which a dominant group deceived themselves about themselves. They thought they were good but in fact they were evil enough to be replaced, because the "Kingdom of God" has not settled on Earth. This book claims that the "Kingdom" is actually not a kingdom because a kingdom implies Christ in the form of one man. "Christ" actually means a plurality of good people who have enough power to enforce God's reign on Earth, until humans will in general be responsible enough to go on without the Law.

The current paradigm, which should be replaced is utilitarianism. It is part of religions, but even worse, it was secularised by being included in Constitutions of for example South-Africa and the United States of America.

Background

What is *intequity*? This question has to be answered, because the neologism was the origin of *Intequinism*. The new words are not included in dictionaries. Previously I thought a definition will be formed with academic research, whilst I am employed by a research institution, but it seems that won't happen, due to the opposing nature of *intequity* to the current world economic system. *Intequity* is currently a descriptive word of something, existing, but it has not entered economic theory. The word *intequity* has been hijacked and is used as business names. *Intequity* names a concept and can be defined as capital of good ideas. I formed the word during 2009 by combining "equity" and "integrity".

Forming the new words *intequity* and *Intequinism* was a direct result of being ostracised. I decided to follow an entrepreneurial career during 1999, by starting a trading business between The People's Republic of China and South-Africa. Instead of aiming at maximum profit, by asking maximum prices, I said then, an aim is a reasonable salary for myself, whilst not charging maximum possible prices. I did not then realise, the capitalist system depends on maximum prices. Non-profit institutions, which pity "the other", are direct results of maximum profit. Without maximum profit, non-profit organisations can also not exist. The impact of maximum profit on society is therefore much wider than just in the economy. Maximum profit also benefits religions. I thought about maximum profit and the reasons for it, the last 17 years and came to the following conclusion. Two reasons for maximum profit exist. The first reason is religious. In Christianity the idea exists, Christ will take everything when "He returns". It is not often discussed, but anyone who *red* St. John's book of Revelation in the Bible, has that idea implanted in his/her mind. The idea in Revelation is inherently linked with capitalism. Another reason for maximum profit is greed, which is interlinked with the idea of Christ, because Christ are used as an excuse for greed. Greedy capitalists claim they make maximum profit to gather everything for Christ's return.

From 1999 to current, I struggled to get financial security, without "success", because of being "too" honest and "too" loving. Bourgeoisie culture sacrifices all extremes, whether it is good or evil, as "not normal". During 2009, when all my savings were depleted, University of South-Africa (UNISA), employed me as a senior lecturer, in the same month I would have been unable to pay for my rent and food, unless I made a loan. During 2017 similar circumstances repeated with another university, but the circumstances were not as opaque as during 2009.

During 1999 I returned to South Africa, after travelling and working as an accountant abroad for 3 years. I saved relatively a lot. Entrepreneurial propaganda influenced me then, and I wanted to invest my savings of the previous three years in a trading business between China and South-Africa. During my three years abroad, I realised, exorbitant profits were being made from all South-Africans, by "middle men" between China and South-Africa. According to Adam Smith's capitalist theory, an opportunity to add value to South-Africa with new value-for-money supplies from China existed, by replacing the "middle men". The idea spread because since then, direct trade with China grew exponentially.

My objective, being non-profit trading, was a mistake, because I counted my chickens before they hatched.

Succeeding with the business was certain in my naive mind because of the big value-for-money savings possible. Chinese motorcycles were not available in South-Africa at the time and I arranged a whole-sale distribution contract with a company from Nanchang called Hongdu. At the time I did not know, entrepreneurship in South-Africa, with the accompanying theory of free markets etc, is theoretical propaganda only. Most people do not realise, ideas are common property and some Western Constitutions promote imparting of ideas as a "human" right, and promote utilitarian development of ideas. The "human" right is understood in opposition to philosophy by Socrates who claimed in Plato's books, Book X of *Republic* and *Ion*, "gods" who are humans, have good ideas. Pagan sacrifices of "gods" and pagan idolatry changed into the Christian idolatrous system, which symbolically sacrifices "God" during each Mass, also called the Eucharist.

The system of sacrificing "God" can be explained simply. The words "ideas", "idols" and "idolatry" are related, because the words originated from the same root. During ancient times, people with good ideas were physically sacrificed, because of the changes, new ideas caused. They were also sometimes regarded mad, and therefore became pharmakos. Forming new ideas was regarded rebellious. The sacrifices apparently were murders of "gods" and "goddesses" by society. It can be understood together with the conviction that "the Creator is" an incorporeal Being and therefore, anyone who is creative, transgresses in the domain of the incorporeal "Creator". This conviction is a functional lie, which motivates the common property status of new ideas. Promotors of utilitarianism further argue, ideas are not formed in minds but by a communal Mind.

Augustine explained in his book *City of God,* for example, the Latin word for a door hinge was the name of the person who formed the idea "hinge". Socrates explained, for example, the word "hygiene" was derived from the name of Apollo's daughter. It can be imagined, the additional work, hygiene caused, was frowned upon by some people, and maybe, the "god's" daughter, who formed the idea was unpopular among other members of society who did not want to live hygienically.

I worked for a UK/German/Chinese joint venture in Beijing, called Wanyuan Draftex, during my time abroad from 1996 to 1999. An old fashioned side car motorcycle, manufactured by Hongdu, I purchased, was sometimes my transport. The Hongdu Chang Jiang (CJ) 750cc M1M gave a lot of fun and it was the first motorcycle I imported to South-Africa for recreational and marketing purposes. The CJ750 looks like a 2nd World War Zundapp/BMW motorcycle and was manufactured with foreign tooling, China imported during or after the 2nd World War. My business plan was to eventually import and distribute many different motorcycles and also to arrange the transfer of the old tooling to South-Africa. In China, consumers regarded the CJ750 as merely transport, and they were tired of the shape. In Cape Town, where I stayed, the CJ750 could have become a recreational motorcycle, similar to a Harley Davidson, especially if the quality could be improved.

I did not realise then, the markets for goods in South-Africa were controlled by powerful groups. That fact was never taught, together with the entrepreneurial propaganda spread by the media and universities.

Recently I realised my plans did not fit well into the current capitalist system, because most non-profit businesses are dependant on donations from maximum profit businesses. My plans to do usual maximum-profit business on a non-profit basis, seemed strange to others. My rebelliousness against maximum profit, which I regarded the main cause of much trouble in the world, convinced me to rebel in other ways, as well. I i.e. wrote a letter to a religious leader in which I expressed my opinion about maximum profit. I did that because religious groups are known to make much profit from trading and I wanted to trade, whilst limiting my own profits. The profits of trading are added to maximum prices of products. My argument was, if I reduce prices and just add enough profit to break even, I could still have a comfortable living. The implications were, no donations would have been paid by my planned business, nor by me, because reduced prices would have been my and my business' contribution to a more equitable society. Pitying, inherent to donations, pushed me away from wanting to donate. I was not a Communist. A big difference between Marxism and *Intequinism* is the hatred Marx had of people with good ideas. His view is comparable to idolatry, which promotes sacrificing of creative people.

During 2001 the South-African Rand depreciated a lot and I decided to not continue the business. I contacted potential investors in the motor industry, to find capital for the business without luck. When I started the business I said the entrepreneurial venture will, if it does not succeed, be forgotten and I will then take a usual job, in order to still have a normal live, whilst hopefully marrying, raising children, etc. My rebellious frustration was however then still active. I think at the time I was already on a black list, because very strange intrusions into my life happened. I moved to Stellenbosch and just wanted a financially secure job as an accountant, somewhere around Stellenbosch, because I liked the scenery there. I could not find work for years and used the time to study music, painting and horse riding. A very serious digestive problem, doctors could not explain, took hold of my life. Anger, due to the circumstances, one day moved me to make another personal mistake. I called a very rich South-African businessman, to complain about maximum profit. I never spoke to him, but one of his employees called me. A lot of frustration, experienced then, was expressed in a long conversation with the representative, to get rid of the frustration. Freedom of speech is a human right and I argued that if more people tell influential business people, the current workings of maximum profit is problematic, because it influence them negatively; it could help to bring a more sustainable system into being. The system needs to change because of the way capital is organised and profits are distributed. Minority shareholders and majority shareholders are treated equally when dividends are declared by maximum profit, public companies. It's a flaw of the law, because maximum profit per individual is not limited.

Without going into details of the extremely challenging circumstances during those years, I will just opine, I was intentionally excluded from the job market. Possibly my digestive problem was caused by poisoning. The statement in St. John's Book of Revelation that when Man overcome poisoning, it will be the end of the world, implies, poisoning in society is much more common than is generally believed. Although I sent hundreds of CV's to potential employers, I was never invited for interviews. During around 2005 I started thinking my circumstances are caused, partly because I did not go to church and did not donate to church affairs. I started donating and going to church and shortly after my choice to become a church goer again I was given work in Bredasdorp. Since around

2001, the terrible digestive problem coincided with rumours being spread that I am gay. In Bredasdorp an argument about sexual matters caused my dismissal and I moved to Johannesburg where the job market was larger. Finding work however was also there not forthcoming, until UNISA employed me during 2009. During the period 1999 to 2009 I did a few contract jobs, but those jobs usually ended in me leaving or being dismissed, due to probable corruption on the horizon.

My theory about the circumstances is as follows: During 1992, when I did my accounting articles, I was falsely diagnosed manic depressive. According to psychiatric theories, manic depressive people are crazy for the rest of their lives and they do not have legal capacity. That means, if a manic depressive person commits fraud, s/he cannot be found guilty. Probably therefore, people with psychiatric diagnoses against them, are put in situations where they are expected to commit fraud, whilst being made pharmakos. Another way to explain it is to say corruption is needed to "oil the capitalist system" and psychiatry plays an important role in the corruption. From 1999 to 2009, due to the circumstances, I was without work most of the time, whilst living on my savings, invested in gold coins, which appreciated in value.

The circumstances made me think of business ideas. Not having a large capital base and not being part of a group, like the Freemasons, or the Church, and also not finding capital, made it impossible to implement the ideas. Many of the ideas I tried to implement, were however imparted to others who implemented it. These circumstances explain one of the biggest problems of the capitalist system. Ideas are common property but capital to develop ideas are not freely available. People who are close to the money generating system can easily favour friends and family to develop good ideas, whilst people who generate ideas can be excluded, because ideas are common property. People who have deceived themselves about themselves cannot generate good ideas because of their deceiving minds. Most people do not understand how the system with regard to ideas work, because the usual comment is, Intellectual Property rights solve the problem. Most people do not know, copyrights and patents can usually not protect ideas. The reason is because ideas can be explained with synonyms and patents are valid territorially. Registering a patent, can, itself, impart a good idea to others in other countries, because patents are transparently open to anyone for perusal. Without going into too much detail about my understanding of Intellectual Property rights, I will just opine, it is extremely difficult to get financial benefit from a good idea, if not part of a group, geared for development, and the best way to protect an idea is with trade secret law.

The summary above of conditions between 1999 and 2009 brings me back to the word *intequity*. From 1999 to 2009 I realised without a doubt that ideas are being systematically imparted from me, but I did not know anything about the workings of the utilitarian Constitutional system. The inclusion of the "human" right called "imparting of ideas" in the Constitution, was not part of my knowledge then. The fact that good new ideas I generated, contributed much to the economy, was clear to me. At the time the press was still very anti ideas. Ideas were portrayed in the press as "only ideas". This has changed and currently, parts of the media promote Truth and new ideas. They however do not respect ideas enough, because often competitions are announced in which creative people are asked to submit their ideas. Only a few winners are chosen and because most people do not realise how valuable good ideas are, they give their ideas away for free, to be developed by utilitarians. The ugly reality was clear to me, due to seeing how others survived, using ideas I generated, whilst being self excluded from the system. Another example of the disrespect towards the generation of new ideas are references by BBC Media to "the disruptors", being a reference to people who innovate new ideas. It is probably a reference to innovators, not developers, because the media industry, benefit together with developers from the utilitarian system of imparting ideas and development thereof.

Something corrupt was going on and, that, imparting of ideas was sometimes stealing ideas, was clear to see. It is legal, to impart ideas, if privacy laws are not broken, but enforcing privacy laws, for example prohibiting digital access to computers, is impossible without very advanced software. Networks and much equity is involved in an organised way, therefore the word *intequity* formed in my mind to express the concept, capital of good ideas, whilst doing research at UNISA from 2009. The research was however not accepted by managing colleagues, due to the opposition the research gives to religious dogma in connection with the economy. At the time a literature study explained some of the religious dogma, relating to fallacious functional religious convictions. My realisations during the literature study was published by *Journal of Emerging Trends in Economics and Management Sciences*. At the end of 2012, UNISA dismissed me, whilst accusing me of thinking I am "God, like Jesus". Due to unbearable victimisation by colleagues, I had to give a warning against a possible brawl, if victimisation did not stop. They regarded my warning as a threatening. Also during 2012, North-West University accepted my registration for an MPhil (Philosophy) degree for continuation of my research about *intequity*. The circumstances made me think of the term Caiaphas Syndrome. When I searched on Google for the term, I saw it was already used in two publications. Thinking of the term self and finding it in two publications, confirmed the logic the term explains.

Creativity

I was watching a television program about the production of a sports car. The planning and precision, which went into the production of the car, is commendable. I am struggling against society to try and get across the idea that creativities are good for a community, therefore, why should "the Creator" be symbolically sacrificed for the good "He" brings. It felt to me as if I am forced to create on my own, by writing this book, whilst I would prefer to work on a group project, which produces something special, like the car they featured in the television program. The car was the centre of interest, and the group activity, which did not include idolatry, whilst cooperating, created the special object, which was not human. First world countries, with their low levels of corruption are far ahead of third world countries, when creativity is considered. They must have a much lower level of Caiaphas Syndrome than third world countries. Kaizen Costing, which is an accounting system for continuous improvement, originated in Japan, and motorcar manufacturers apply it. Due to Caiaphas Syndrome in the work place, applying Kaizen Costing, however, is not always possible. The old company ISCOR, which manufactured iron in South-Africa had a system whereby people with good ideas were paid bonuses. Mittal, the new company does not apply the old ISCOR system anymore. The Mittal policy is a good example of utilitarianism, which replaced deontology.

How are good ideas imparted from all over the world to sustain first world production. Can it be explained? Only in an hypothesis, which cannot be proven empirically. Idolators impart good ideas of third world citizens and sell it on to production entities in first world countries. John

Perry Barlow mentioned, the idea which originated personal computers, probably originated in South-East Asia. He also mentioned how ideas are being traded for ideas, without using the exchange of money.

Local ideas should be controlled, to first benefit all citizens locally.

Circumstances show the effects of culture on creativity. In uncreative cultures creativity is equated with femininity and honest creative men are not allowed to work, without being called gay.

Philosophy

MPhil (Philosophy) studies at North-West University made a big contribution to understanding the utilitarian evil paradigm, in connection with my circumstances since 1999. North-West University is a Christian University in the Calvinist Reformed School. Their philosophy focuses a lot on the ideas of creation and its influence on order. It is based on non-reductionist ontology. By non-reductionist ontology is meant, a realist view of the whole, without focusing on an essence. They refer to aspectual views, instead of to essence of dialectical philosophy. Instead of reducing reason to one field, for example economics, like Marx did, they say many considerations are relevant to see realistic wholes. Non-reductionism eventually influenced me, together with Platonic/Socratic ideas, to identify two important ideas, which according to *Intequinism* must be respected by some people above themselves. The two ideas are Truth and Love. Without having the two ideas, respected above enough people, an economy cannot be sustainable.

Up to the end of 2012, when UNISA dismissed me, I consciously placed one idea, namely Truth above me, because, according to my upbringing, Truth was the essence. My subconscious respect for the idea Love, moved me to give a warning to UNISA about the possibility of snapping if victimisation did not stop. Between Truth only and Christian conviction, too many contradictions existed. The influence of the ideas Truth and Love, was stronger than Christian conviction, according to which one man can be "God". The conviction is simply not true and these days Christianity in my view is idolatry. It was Truth, and the negative view relating to truth in Christianity, which moved me to officially end my membership of Christianity. Christianity often has negativity towards Truth, due to Christian convictions about Truth and singularity of "the individual". Main stream Christians made "love" their essence. The argument that honest people think they each "is God", and how that affects behaviour of Christians negatively, had a big influence on my decision to resign as Christian. The unbearable victimisation at UNISA, which I had to give a warning against, due to Love, later, whilst studying non-reductionist philosophy, made me realise consciously, the idea Love was also relevant. Love with a capital L and "love" however have different definitions. Dictionary definitions for "love", usually correspond more to eros than agape.

Why are these two ideas, Truth and Love relevant? Basically my argument is, without these two ideas, respected above enough people, *intequity* cannot exist. *Intequity* is necessary for continued sustainability. I defined *intequity* as capital of good ideas. Comprehending what capital is, is not problematic. Equity, for those who do not understand accounting, is a type of capital. Equity represents what business owners own. It is their share of businesses. Businesses are partly financed with debt as well, another form of capital. *Intequity* values are currently included in equity valuations but should be abstracted from equity to understand better, how *values* are formed. *Intequity* values can be calculated by doing *honery* tests, which I will write a little more about later.

Consider how equity is currently formed. Ideas originate first. Then capital is raised and used to develop ideas by employing labour and utilising natural resources. Without ideas, nothing would form in the economy, except natural organic growth. According to capitalist entrepreneurial economic theory, equity is formed when four production factors, namely; capital, labour, natural resources and entrepreneurship combines. Ideas are not considered. I realised, this theory, which is taught at universities is utilitarian, which *Intequinism* opposes. The term "religious utilitarianism" is also used. To those without a philosophy background, utilitarianism basically is the following: The philosophy argues the reductionist objective, which influence our doings, is the greatest amount of happiness. Important though, happiness, being the objective, is not of self or of another. It is happiness of a group, self belongs to. It is further argued, that, happiness of the group is caused by consuming utilities. It can sound logical and the utilitarian idea also influenced me around 1999 because then I had kind of utilitarian convictions, aiming for happiness of the group (all South-Africans), by supplying new value-for-money products at reduced prices. The utilitarian reality about relationships between groups and individuals however then was not understood by me, partly because my previous studies were not in the humanities. The problem with utilitarianism is, it does not include all relevant people with universal Love, because some people in the community are treated as scape goats and the profane. Utilitarianism is dependent on division, because the philosophy presupposes the existence of scape goats who are separate from the group. The group's happiness, excluding "the Other's" happiness, is the objective. The best known example of how utilitarianism works, was made known by Christianity. Jesus was identified as the profane and Caiaphas argued he should be sacrificed, because his sacrifice will cause more happiness for the group. This is how utilitarianism works, because "the Creator", who die for the sins of Christians, are creative "profane" people, whose ideas are developed in the capitalist utilitarian entrepreneurial system. Christians who deceive themselves about themselves cannot generate good enough ideas for their survival, due to their tainted minds, therefore they are dependent on imparting ideas from the profane, whilst excluding the profane. I was and still am one of the profane, who is being targeted, because of my honesty. My mind is not tainted enough to have lost my creative ability, like most Christians' minds. Due to my honesty, good ideas are imparted from me and developed, whilst excluding me from the system. The most recent example is an idea I shared with several entrepreneurs and bureaucrats, which will eventually contribute billions to economies, but I am not included in development work, although I asked to be included. The idea is simply that diversified businesses can save almost their whole salary bill, by using their own currencies. In stead of crediting bank when they pay salaries they can credit their own currency, employees can exchange for goods of the business. Supermarkets can apply the idea very easily.

What is missing in the utilitarian economic philosophical theory, summarised above? The four production factors in the theory are capital, labour, natural resources, and entrepreneurship. What about identifying ideas and networking separately? According to *Intequinism*, the production factor entrepreneurship in relation to equity, should be split between generating ideas and networking, because both are relevant at entrepreneurship, but the tasks are performed by people with very different outlooks on life. Currently ideas are common property, due to religious utilitarianism and people who are good at networking, appropriate and develop most good ideas, whilst excluding originators of good ideas. The fact that ideas are utilitarian common property according to the law, is usually disputed because of others' limited knowledge of patents and copyrights. One of the reasons, ideas are common property is, according to utilitarian philosophy, ideas should be duplicated as wide as possible, because then utilities are developed for wide consumption, which causes happiness. Ideas can be distinguished from physical goods. An idea can be implemented in different ways and patents are registered on the physical things, which use ideas. The analytical utilitarian argument, further promoting the common property status of ideas, is that all good ideas originate from incorporeal "God" and therefore humans cannot claim remuneration or inclusion for their ideas, according to the law. An employee can i.e. not claim a bonus for contributing with good ideas to business of an employer. Such bonuses are discretionary. The conviction, which caused the circumstances according to the law, is rooted in idolatry.

In reality ideas originate before development. Then money is printed or raised to employ people who develop ideas. Current capitalist entrepreneurial economic theory does not mention ideas, because the only four production factors considered are capital, labour, natural resources and entrepreneurship. Entrepreneurship does not value ideas. The result is that people who have money, readily available, have too much financial security, because they develop most good ideas, although they did not originate those ideas. When someone, with a good idea wants to raise finance, financiers are not obligated to finance the person with the good idea. They can easily finance another person to implement the idea, because ideas are common property.

Imparting of ideas further happens when security agencies spy with digital technology. Writing an idea in digital form is risky because creative people cannot know who is transgressing into their private spaces, i.e. on personal computers, especially if it is national authorities who are involved in the transgressions under the guise of safety and security or public interest. Safety and security theories, combined psychiatry and accusations that honest others think they each is Christ and therefore pose terrorist threats. Creative people are regarded as worthwhile sources to spy upon and the safety and security excuse is misused. It was for example reported that Tesla's work was nationalised by the USA government, whilst transgressing into his privacy. Laws, which regard certain people, like well known public figures, as public property, is another negative implication of utilitarian philosophy.

Truth

The most basic difference between philosophers, relates to the word Truth, and defining the idea Truth or not. Most philosophers prefer eventual coherence but they disagree about the way towards coherence. Some say communicating correspondences will lead to coherence and others say functional lies, intentionally, must be used on the way to coherence. Correspondence can be defined with different definitions, especially with regard to the influence concepts have. Different definitions of concepts have the biggest negative effect on correspondent communication, and according to *Intequinism*, the fact of different definitions, especially of concepts, is no reason to reject the correspondence theory of Truth. Knowing the reality; different definitions for things (including concepts) exist, motivates to be more honest when communicating, on the way to coherence. Thus, the basic difference between the modernist and post-modernist theses is how the idea Christ is perceived. Modernists regard the returned Christ as a living corporeal group and post-modernists regard Christ as a single human being, dead or alive.

Previous research from 2009 to 2011, about Accounting of ideas, confirmed to me that honesty partly causes creativity. A correlation between the most successful companies and least corrupt economies, according to an International Corruption Index exists. Honest people have more good ideas than dishonest people and dishonest people are better at networking than honest people. That research was published by *Journal of Emerging Trends in Economics and Management Sciences* in a paper called "Management Accounting of Intellectual Creations". The conclusion can logically be inferred when considering, forming new good ideas happens when previous known realities are combined in minds to form new ideas. Thinking can be compared to, and represent processes of physically putting things together to form new physical wholes. If minds include only realities, obviously such minds will be better at thinking creatively than minds, which also include fallacies. Aristotle explained it when he said a thought is false when it cannot be used in a process of "assembly". He also wrote, a knowledgeable man is a man who knows how to use lies functionally. In ancient philosophy, being knowledgeable and lying were closely interlinked. Aristotle's view was and still is taught and accepted, for example with Machiavellian views. The relation between Aristotle's thought about "assembly" and religious assemblies is relevant, because Aristotle had the biggest influence on Roman Catholic Scholastic thought, before the Enlightenment. Logically, lying improves memory, but reduces creative thought, because of false puzzle pieces, which are remembered. Creative thought does not necessarily mean creativity in conjunction with negative Marxist views about creativity, often equated with "progress" in post-modern Philosophy of Science. Good creative thought addresses totality and progress must be considered in conjunction with the consequences it has on all, including owners of defunct technologies, as far as possible.

Views about "God", also called "the Creator" has a long history, which can be traced back to ancient philosophy. God, Truth and creativity have been considered together in an idolatrous sense since Pre-Socratic times. Socrates explained his view as follows: "And surely we must value truthfulness highly. For if we were right when we said just now that falsehood is no use to the gods and only useful to men as a kind of medicine, it's clearly a kind of medicine that should be entrusted to doctors and not to laymen. . . It will be for the rulers of our city, then, if anyone, to use falsehood in dealing with citizen or enemy for the good of the State; no one else must do so." (Plato 350BCb: 389a) Although Socrates here, promoted Truth, his statement is rejected because it allows the use of functional lies by rulers.

Socrates further explained in Book X of *the Republic* and in *Ion*, that gods and goddesses had good ideas. He also swore in the "name of the dog", whilst Athens's state "god" was Zeus. Whether Socrates was sometimes referring to Zeus is not clear. Socrates's philosophy thus partly explained the negative influences of idolatry. The dogs were the creative people who were isolated and ostracised by society. Zeus stayed in a cave on Crete according to Plato's book *Laws*, which could mean he was also ostracised. Theuth, who discovered the alphabet, which was rejected by Amen, according to Socrates, could be Zeus, who knows. Diogenes of Sinope was an ostracised person in Athens. He lived in a wine jar close to Athens's market. Diogenes was a cynic; the word cynic was derived from a Greek word meaning dog. Nietzsche's parable about dead "God" is very similar to a story about Diogenes who went to the market one morning early with a lantern. He shouted, the people should show him an honest man because he could not find an honest man. Most honest men were probably dead or depressed and without work, and therefore, slept late. Socrates's view of God, being partly humans who live like dogs, is also found in Kearney's Philosophy of Religion. Jesus's vagrant lifestyle shows the same circumstances in Christian conviction. Christian convictions however led to current economic systems, with rampant vagrancy. Vagrancy is justified with the functional conviction in Christlike vagrancy. The return of

Christ in a singular sense is functional and shall never happen, because no person, given Christlike authority, will ever agree to being God, but in the meantime, until the next revolution, which will adjust political theory with actualities, vagrancy is accepted as part of Christian convictions. Socrates and Plato, his hermeneutic publisher, influenced Christianity much, especially before and after the Middle Age.

The problems relate further to religions because Aquinas (1273) referred cosmologically to "God Himself Who cannot lie". Descartes (1641: 19) wrote: "From this it is manifest that He cannot be a deceiver, since the light of nature teaches us that fraud and deception necessarily proceed from some defect."

Honesty in religion and philosophy relates to "gods" and "goddesses", which is a sensitive issue many do not like to discuss.

Nietzsche (1886: 156) wrote: "Honesty – granted that this is our virtue, from which we cannot get free, we free spirits – well, let us labour at it with all love and malice and not weary of 'perfecting' ourselves in our virtue, the only one we have: may its brightness one day overspread this ageing culture and its dull, gloomy seriousness like a gilded azure mocking evening glow! And if our honesty should one day none the less grow weary, and sigh, and stretch its limbs, and find us too hard, and like to have things better, easier, gentler, like an agreeable vice: let us remain hard, we last of the Stoics! And let us send to the aid of our honesty whatever we have of devilry in us – our disgust at the clumsy and casual, our 'nimitur in vetitum', our adventurer's courage, our sharp and fastidious curiosity, our subtlest, most disguised, most spiritual will to power and world-overcoming which wanders avidly through all the realms of the future – let us go to the aid of our 'god' with all our 'devils'! It is probable that we shall be misunderstood and taken for what we are not: but what of that! People will say: 'Their "honesty" - is their devilry and nothing more!' But what of that! And even if they were right! Have all gods hitherto not been such devils grown holy and been rebaptized?" Amazing what good language use can do, isn't it. Unfortunately language was my worst subject at school and I cannot write like this. Why I ended up writing, only God can explain.

Nietzsche was right when he wrote the Christian singular weak "God" is dead, whilst motivating wills to power, via honesty. He was however a bit idolatrous in the above quote, whilst referring to "our 'god'" in the present tense. Having "'god'" in inverted commas shows he did not regard it his terminology and thereby he rejects the use of the word "god" with regard to present and future, whilst recognising the historical use of the word "god", and the implications the historical use has for the present and future. Nietzsche respected the idea Truth but he did not respect Love, which can be seen in his book *The Antichrist*, where he specifically rejects Kant's categorical imperative. Kant's categorical imperative states; before doing something people should consider what the effect on the world will be if all people do the same. Kant's categorical imperative was an expansion of the idea Love. Western culture supports my opinion because Kant's categorical imperative is accepted in Western Philosophy of Law. Nietzsche promoted the law in *The Antichrist* but it was law of privilege, not universal Law (Love) of equal rights.

The Greek word "chrestotes" appears eight times in the New Testament and was translated as "goodness", "kindness", "integrity" etc. of God (BST). In Plato's works "chrestotes" was translated with "honesty" (Plato 350BC: 412e). Honesty of God is partly the reason of the functional argument—you think you are God—Caiaphas used in his utilitarian argument to sacrifice Jesus. The utilitarian argument is further motivated by Greek words, which indicate the usefulness of honesty to society, albeit in an utilitarian sense. Currently Christians use the same accusation to isolate honest people, whilst imparting ideas and developing it.

The ontological realisation; each person has different definitions for words of definitions for words of definitions ad infinitum, motivates to be more honest; to consider others' meanings of words, when communicating. Creativity is a result of honesty, and creativity is important to attain sustainability of large populations. Malthus explained that due to overpopulation and non-sustainability, cyclical disasters reduce population numbers, to restore balance between population numbers and available resources. Boserup explained that Malthus's thesis is wrong and with enough creativity humans can live sustainably.

Currently, due to Caiaphas Syndrome, enough creativity is not allowed to cause the sustainability Boserup referred to, because "the Creator" are not allowed to work on the development of their good creative ideas. Good ideas are common property and the capitalist economic system is geared for imparting of ideas and development, whilst isolating "the dog". Marx explained his hatred for people who innovate ideas in his book *Capital Volume One*, whilst calling only labour "the creator". Between Marxism and capitalist utilitarianism a close connection exists.

The bottom line is, without necessary good ideas Malthus's theory, which includes war, is relevant but with Boserup's theory in mind, population growth can stabilise in balance with resources, without revolutionary upheavals.

Love

Love is the other idea, necessary above enough humans for *intequity* to exist. Creativity works best in group form, but often, before development, creative ideas originate at individuals. Due to changes to the status quo, creativities cause the outlawing of individuals, who each is always weak. Creative people therefore need to be protected against Caiaphas Syndrome of groups. Idolatrous utilitarian isolation of "the individual" whilst "His" ideas are being imparted and developed is a methodology, the idea Love does not allow, because no human is a god or a goddess, who will be saved by supernatural means. The Law should protect people against Caiaphas Syndrome. Pagan blood sacrifice of creators was replaced by the Eucharist, nihilism and isolation of creative people. Creative people should be respected for the contributions they make to society with good ideas, without being influenced by idolatrous theses. Idolatry, basically is the sacrifice of creative people and the praising of them after the sacrifices.

Love, it seems developed as a balancing idea, against Truth. Truth can become despotic when rulers and powerful people have the right to destroy competition, whilst being honest about it. The Sophists therefor started to promote social contract theory, which relates to universal Laws and Love. Not-doing evil to others is also the main idea of the Ten Commandments. When Jesus was asked what Love is, he replied it is a summary of the law and the prophets. Thomas Hobbes explained clearly in his book *Leviathan* how social contract theory developed from the idea to do to others as selves want to be done to. That idea cannot exist without not-doing evil, which is prior to doing good.

It is important to distinguish at least between two types of Love. The first is not-doing evil to others like selves do not want to be done to. Not-doing is universal because not-doing evil can be done to all people in the world. Not-doing evil is international Love. Love, which is also doing good to fellow citizens, usually more locally applicable, became more relevant in a nationalistic sense. It is not possible to do good to all people in the world. How wide Love should be applied is problematic in Christianity because Christianity does not address universal not-doing evil, except in the Old Testament in the Ten Commandments. It is only doing good to others, which is usually addressed by Christians. Doing good to family and friends sometimes follows doing evil to "the other". Paul is sometimes mentioned to argue against the Law, which relates to not-doing evil to others and the Ten Commandments. A New Testament argument is sometimes, Christians are not subject to the Law. It is however a contradiction to interpret the New Testament as such because the Law and Love are related. Logically the arguments by Paul against the Law, can mean that humans should apply Love and the Law of not-doing evil to others self, without the need of Love being enforced with the Law. Another explanation could relate to doing good. John Stuart Mill, a utilitarian, can be credited with an idea he promoted; the Law should not enforce what people should do. Universal Law only enforces what people should not do. This idea is better developed in the East than the West, which can be seen in the following religious quotations, which usually refer to not-doing: Kearney (2011:150) referred to the following passages:

"*Zoroastrianism*: "Do not do unto others whatever is injurious to yourself" (Sahyast-na-Shayast, 13:29)

Buddhism: "Treat not others in ways that you yourself would find hurtful" (Udana-Varga 5:18)"

"*Confucianism*: "One word that sums up the basis of all good conduct … loving kindness. Do not do to others what you do not want done to yourself" (Confucius, Analects 15:23).

Hinduism: "This is the sum of duty: do not do to others what would cause pain if done to you" (Mahabharata 5:1517)."

Thomas Hobbes (1651: 223) wrote in *Leviathan* that "we" need "the terrour of some Power" to enforce the social contract because all of us do not subscribe to "(in summe) *doing to others, as wee would be done to*". Until all people have the self control to stop themselves from doing to others like they do not want to be done to, a need for sovereigns, who enforce the Law and Love, will exist. Until political systems allow access by all people, to acquire freedom, whilst respecting Truth and Love above themselves, disrespect of the two ideas will happen, for survival and "reproduction".

In Constitutions, academic freedom gives academics the right to freely create and oppose the status quo and they may not be victimised and harassed. In the USA especially, tenure further protects academics against idolatrous sacrificing by idolators. Other countries, which do not apply tenure in line with protection of creative individuals, can learn from those circumstances.

Beauty

Beauty is an important idea but beauty does not have the same importance as Truth and Love for society. Although beauty can bring much benefit to society and to individuals each, beauty can be an opposing force to Truth and Love, because the more beautiful people are, the more difficult it can be to be honest and loving. The temptations beautiful people experience, to be deceiving and non-loving can be enormous. Beautiful people can enthral others with their beauty, which makes it easy for them to misuse the natural gift they were born with.

On the other hand due to natural respect, for beauty, beautiful people can be honest and loving. They have perhaps the least reason to be dishonest and non-loving, to survive, in capitalist states.

God

Caiaphas Syndrome causes accusations that living honest loving people think they each is God. The accusation causes dishonesty and hatred, which cause disorder. If all human beings were honest loving people, little need for the Law would exist, but all people are not honest and loving, therefore God gave the Law to replace disorder with order.

God is not, but are the most important Being and are understood in connection with the ideas Truth and Love above. Belief in God gives the power to respect Truth and Love above selves. Power to trust, is needed to respect Truth and Love above self, because temptations, which are forthcoming to people who respect Truth and Love above themselves, happen. Trust in God is more likely if God are defined as partly a human powerful group who enforces the Law. God are "the Creator". Creativities exist, therefore God exist.

When things start to go wrong and selves each do not have the power to control the circumstances, trust in stronger Being than one's own being is necessary. God have Being, selves can trust, because God are powerful. God is not a singular being. God are all living honest loving people plus Logos. The capital G of God implies plural form, similar to other instances when letters are capitalised to indicate plural form. Another example is "Man", which indicates plural form.

The obvious similarity between the words God, god, goddess, gods and goddesses raises the question whether honest loving people are gods and goddesses. The answer is categorically no, because the words god and goddess relate to history and idolatry. *Intequinism* rejects idolatry completely. No man can be a god and no woman can be a goddess. The words god and goddess can be understood in many different ways. The words can refer, for example, to strong, tall, beautiful and/or intelligent people. Sometimes people with supernatural powers are called gods and goddesses. To comprehend *Intequinism,* Socrates's definition of gods and goddesses are important because his definition was especially relevant at modern religion. Idolatry and sacrificing people go hand in hand. People are sacrificed by idolators and when they are dead they are portrayed as gods and goddesses. Idolatry is a business, which parasitises others by putting them intentionally in difficult circumstances, partly, to later tell their stories in the media, for profit. Idolatry is also a way to get rid of competition when honest loving people oppose the status quo.

Different definitions for words of definitions for words of definitions exist, ad infinitum. Therefore when Truth is considered, the correspondence of words with reality, depends on, from whose viewpoints words are considered. A speaker and listener can have completely different meanings attached to a word. This problem is relevant at the word God, because definitions for the word differ. True correspondences can be equated with words, especially when physical things are referred to, which give meaning to words. Examples are "table" or "chair", being used literally. Does the word God have a true meaning? Different meanings for God exist because God are for some, partly physical and for others God is wholly incorporeal. Due to viewing for a wholly incorporeal metaphysical God, or the view for the partly metaphysical part of God, different definitions for God exist. It is also said no definition for God exists. Aquinas wrote that, with his cosmological proof for God in opposition to ontological proofs for God, which is based on definitions.

For me, power is inherently part of the meaning of the word God, therefore the thesis; one man can be God, is irrational. If it ever happens that a large part of the world say one living man is God, in the sense of a returned Christ, that man will say he is not God, according to the Book of Revelation. In the prediction his view is rational and the people who claim he is God is irrational, because one man is powerless. If the word God however merely meant an important leader, then it could make sense, but the word has a much wider meaning than that.

The wider meaning of the word God, than merely, historical god (deified person), came about partly because of cosmological views for God, like Aristotle's and Aquinas's. Such cosmological views are not rational, but it did however make a contribution to comprehending what the word God actually means. Rationality is dependent on definitions. When cosmological views are used, by Christians, to make the profane "sick", like Nietzsche explained in his book *The Antichrist*, a way to counter Christian parasitism is, focusing on ontological definitions, and focusing on the difference between such definitions and cosmological metaphoric references to "Father", "Mother" and "Son". When definitions are used during discussions about God, cosmological viewers stop reasoning, or they become aggressive, because they reason pragmatically, using force, without definitions. They do not have definitions as part of their convictions. Their references to God are primarily functional idolatry to influence people who are honest and loving.

Totality and "One"

According to Parmenides, order of totality, which he called One, is dependent on honesty. He thus identified the correlation between orderly societies and honesty. Unfortunately cosmological philosophers started to correlate Parmenides's idea of One with "One" human being. They argue the One cosmos will favour the "One" human being at the end of time. No evidence for such an event in history exists and because history repeats, a rational thought is to reject this cosmological idea with ontological realisations. Ontological realisations are more rational because of nominalist beliefs, which balance philosophical realism. Sometimes philosophical realism, with modern Philosophy of Science promote deceit, for "coherence". According to an ontological view, correspondences will lead to coherence. It seems nature does not allow phenomena in minds, which relate too closely with reality, because dreams disentangle real memories, by forcing unreal memories into minds. That does not mean humans should join nature in putting false puzzle pieces in minds, with functional lies.

Totality, the whole and all, are words to refer with philosophical realism to the universe. In philosophical terms, realism means comprehension of a larger picture than only the here and now. The word realism can be deceiving, because without having studied philosophy, realism can have a nominalist meaning. Nominalism refers to a recognition of reality, which excludes universals. According to nominalists a universal idea, like gravity is not believed to be universally applicable because experiences are situated in finite spaces and times. With nominalism the here and now is the only reality. A presupposition of nominalism is, it cannot be accepted that universal phenomena are always and everywhere applicable. Nominalism is a valuable ism to comprehend in opposition to realism, because philosophical realism can sometimes lead to hubris. Gravity, for example, at sea level does not cause the same weight for the same mass, than high up on mountains. It proves the value of nominalist realisations.

"The new philosophy of science" threatens objective functions of language. Incommensurabilities are results of attributing corresponding truth values to theories, because when that happens, every theory has an own "reality" connected to it. Sometimes other theories than the theory of corresponding truths then become idealistically "True". (Botha, 1988:42) Sometimes "the big picture", a totalitarianism, subjectively experienced, can become "the truth", whilst disrespecting the correspondence theory of the idea Truth.

Knowing that selves each cannot know everything is an important realisation to be rational. According to *Intequinism* the most accurate picture of the largest whole can be recognised by living honest loving people as a group. An argument exists, which claims, the most accurate understanding of the whole can only be done by one person at a time. This argument is one of the arguments, which favours convictions that God can be "One" human. According to *Intequinism* the world is to complicated and diverse for "One" person to have a holistic understanding of the whole.

It follows; the most realistic recognition of the whole by leaders is done in an aspectual way by a group, for decision making purposes. Specialists of different fields combine their knowledge for effective decision making, and by way of voting in a group, take good decisions. They all should respect the idea Truth as correspondence, otherwise each theory becomes a reality in itself and one reality is not considered. If Truth is not respected, the different views of different specialists will oppose without being resolved peacefully.

A problem of *Intequinism* is, it is a philosophy for groups, because it promotes creativities and sustainability in group form. If the philosophy is applied by individuals each, without other individuals together, in a group, the good effects, possible for a group, can be turned on its head for individuals each. An individual only, who applies *Intequinism* can be disadvantaged seriously by society due to Caiaphas Syndrome. My life is a good example of the negative effects, the ideas Truth and Love can have on individuals each, when others do not share respect for those two good ideas. The same happened to countless other people, and the struggle continues, because of honesty and consequential wills to power, Nietzsche explained. It is a pity Nietzsche did not promote Love.

Maximum Profit

Maximum profit enlarges the differences between the rich and the poor, which cause problems. It is important to, for example, have a healthy difference between the salaries of management and lower paid workers of a corporation. Maximum profit is idolatrous, because utilitarian imparting of ideas and development of those ideas, whilst excluding Socrates's "gods", from earning and working, is part of the entrepreneurial system. Ideas, which are common property according to the law, are imparted and developed by international corporations, which have access to readily available capital. Recently BBC World News reported, the eight richest people in the world owns as much as the 50% poorest people in the world. I would not be surprised if it is more than 50%. *Intequinism* was caused partly by my opposition against maximum profit, and the consequences, which started around 2000.

The Communist revolutionary thesis about sudden change for good is not logical. Such changes happened because humans did not, before such changes happened, act rationally, by allowing gradual changes. When sudden total redistribution of wealth happens, according to the Communist thesis, for example, experience showed, production can be affected negatively. Logically, redistribution of wealth can cause wider financial security, which could improve order, due to less transgressions of the Law, to live, but sudden increases in production, to allow wider consumption, are not possible. A more equal distribution of wealth suddenly, cannot be mirrored with a larger production output suddenly, therefore gradual distribution of wealth, which can be mirrored by gradual improvements of production outputs, make sense.

Recently, after watching videos on Youtube in which influential people opined about the problem, it became clear, various influential rich people have the opinion that too many people exist and that Malthus's theory is currently relevant. After however looking at the Earth's surface and the space, humans occupy, it looked more like Boserup's theory is currently true. That means production can increase gradually to the right level. Private property however is a problem because much privately owned land is not productively used, therefore nationalisation of unproductive land in One world could be relevant. A redistribution of wealth, for example, instituting a limit on individual wealth, should, because of practicality, relating to mirrored production output, be phased in over the same period production and consequential possible consumption, mirror wealth distribution.

Intequinism's opposition's philosophy is as follows in my view. They argue, maximum profit is warranted until Christ returns, who will take everything. Who is this Christ though and can such a person exist? In my view the ideas of the Christ and Messiah, which are related, are functional ideas, not based on reality, and motivates maximum profit. Maximum profit, which causes much problems, will therefore not be overcome until enough people realise the idea about the Christ and Messiah is a functional lie. Another thought is, maximum profit will be overcome when the actual "Christ" or "Messiah" appears, but it is impossible, because such a man will acknowledge the truth, he is not Christ or the Messiah. The only way thus that maximum profit can be overcome is when everybody realises the idea about "One" human, was a functional lie, which influenced society.

Pitying in a negative way, is part of the maximum profit system. First conglomerates make maximum profit in ways, which disrespect Love and Truth and then the poor are pitied. The economic system will work better if a cap is placed on individual wealth. When a person reaches the level, which could be high enough to allow good lives, s/he can decide whether s/he wants to keep on working without increasing his/her wealth, or whether s/he wants to expand his/her knowledge by studying, doing sport or practising art, for example. Putting a cap on individual wealth is a policy, which can only be decided on, after wide discussion. Yesterday, 16 November 2017, three relevant things occurred. It was the United Nations international Philosophy Day. Leonardo Da Vinci's painting of Christ, the *Salvator Mundi*, was auctioned for 450 million United States Dollars, a once off profit of a few hundred million Dollars. The first draft of this book was sent for language editing and possible voluntary comment. The once off profit on the sale of the painting has to be considered when caps on individual wealth is considered. The point is, one person cannot decide on such a cap, if it is at all advisable, because one person cannot consider all the relevant factors.

Communism also opposed maximum profit, but Marx made one big mistake. He opposed new ideas because he argued new ideas take jobs away. He did not consider the effect good politics can have on progress, by working together with good new ideas, to balance circumstances. Good politics should work in conjunction with good new ideas. Possible future joblessness, due to innovation must be addressed with new political ideas. Innovation must be controlled, albeit not by sacrificing "the individual". Marx and Engels ridiculed the Bauer brothers in their book *The Holy Family*, which could mean they suffered of Caiaphas Syndrome. Good ideas are not necessarily "progressive". A good idea is to control creativity and progress in conjunction with new political theories.

An important consideration is, how new ideas can be controlled, due to the "disruptive" effect new ideas can have on societies. A good example is the changing financial security of Arab states, due to new technologies, in place of oil energy. Ideas can effectively, only be controlled in One world, by cooperation among different territories and respect for all human beings, without making too many distinctions among human beings.

When Truth and Love are not respected, via maximum profit and pitying, groups within groups centralise wealth, whilst excluding formation of new wealth and *intequible* distribution of wealth in a wide sense. Who is thy neighbour? International not-doing evil to all, means all people are international neighbours. National Love; doing good to fellow citizens, means national citizens are closer neighbours than international neighbours. International Love; not-doing evil, is prior and more important than national Love. Family and friends, whether they are internationally or nationally located are even closer than fellow citizens. Disrespecting International Love (not-doing evil to others) in order to do good (National Love) to family, will be transgressions of Law and therefore, people's philosophies and systems should change.

The *Caiaphaci*

We all make mistakes, and sin, and part of freedom of speech is to give our opinions about others' mistakes lovingly, without attacking others or ostracising others. Justifying ostracising of individuals on utilitarian grounds without discussing differences and listening to opinions, is not respect for Love. Love is an all inclusive idea. The pagan utilitarian idea of sacrificing the profane, whilst imparting their ideas and developing those ideas for utilitarian happiness, changed with Christianity into symbolic sacrifice (isolation) of the profane. With Christianity more freedom to creative people were allowed. They were not physically murdered with blood sacrifices. Currently the symbolic sacrifice of the profane, with the Eucharist should be annulled. An argument by Christians is that the Eucharist signifies Jesus's self-sacrifice, which is not true because he was sacrificed by others. Him staying in Jerusalem and not fleeing, does not mean self-sacrifice. It means that he was tired of moving and wanted to become part of Jerusalem's society, but was not accepted. Realising that he was ostracised and used as a utilitarian sacrifice, he could have meant, he should be the last utilitarian sacrifice and in future, creative people should not be sacrificed any more because of a societal change. Unfortunately his hope did not realise, because utilitarian sacrifices of the profane continued into the current era. Usual pagan blood sacrifices changed to symbolic Eucharistic sacrifice, which is not as severe, but the problem of sacrificing the profane for utilitarian benefits still exists. With regard to current economic utilitarian development of ideas in connection with religious rituals, the actuality is that Eucharistic nihilism causes a blind acceptance of vagrancy in Western

Economies. The required origination of new ideas to sustain large populations in coherence with Boserup's theory is inhibited by the symbolic sacrificing of "the Creator". One of the main reasons for the establishment of the Free Masons, for example, was the imparting of ideas and development, in favour of their members. If men's and women's consciences prohibit them from being part of assemblies like Free Masonry and Christianity, which promote utilitarian imparting of ideas and development, what are we to do? After all, utilitarian imparting of ideas was included in national Constitutions.

The ideas Truth and Love are above Constitutions and the lies, which are necessary to continue utilitarian imparting of ideas and development, whilst isolating the profane; will be exposed as time goes on, for improvement, because large populations cannot do without necessary creative ideas, the profane generate.

Big troublemakers are the prophets who promote the return of Christ in a singular sense. Without that conviction it would not be possible to accuse "the individual" (individuals) of thinking they each is God. That accusation is the main argument for isolating people and calling them mad. Religious groups are the cause of such alienating accusations. It is not only the prophets who are to blame, because also, those who have the conviction of a singular Christ, without prophesying it, can argue in an idolatrous sense for sacrificing people, in favour of their idol of the future.

On the other hand, who are causing this searching for a saviour? What do people want to be saved from, which make most people reach out to fallacious praising of a saviour. It looks as if a really evil force is behind it. Is it real or is it all in the minds of idolators. Two professors who were victimising me at UNISA said very weird things. One said his family is in danger. Another professor said "they are cannibals". It looks as if a group of evil people influence others, by scaring them, by making them think something awful will happen with them or their families if they do not victimise the profane. A common reaction when I mention these circumstances, is that it is all in my mind and it does not really exist. There are however, after 17 years of experiencing these circumstances many examples I can give to support this opinion. The bottom line is, everything that happened points to a group who harasses society into submission. If people give opposition, they get ostracised/outlawed and then this harassing group impart ideas, the outlawed/ostracised come up with, under stress. The harassing group of evil people, I call the Caiaphaci, tell stories about the ostracised/outlawed, in movies and books about outlaws. Sometimes the stories form cults, out of which, for example, Christianity grew. Religious/pastoral hermeneutics, which is an acceptable part of academic life is one of the problems. Roberts (1995:193) wrote: "It was at Athens, too, that public opinion was convulced, on the eve of the Sicilian Expedition, by the mysterious and ominous mutilation of certain public statues, the 'Hermae', or busts of Hermes. The disasters which followed were attributed by some to this sacrilege. Socrates the Athenian philosopher who became, thanks to his pupil Plato, the archetypal figure of the man of intellect, and left as a maxim the view that 'the unexamined life is not worth living', offended the pieties of his state and was condemned to die for it by his fellow-citizens; he was also condemned for questioning received astronomy. It does not seem that similar trials took place elsewhere, but they imply a background of popular superstition which must have been more typical of the Greek community than the presence of a Socrates." Socrates was followed and his actions and words were recorded, similar to what happened with Jesus. It seems that a group who practice hermeneutics blindly, made Hermes their "god" and they have a much wider influence in society than is generally known.

A solution is realising the reality; no man or woman can be the god or the goddess, now and in the future; no other derivation of using the word god, with regard to the present and future, is good, because doing that invokes idolatrous ideas with its concomitant sacrifices, whether physical or symbolic. Those words should have only historical meaning. The word God is understood as a plurality of living people, which the capital G indicates. Being part of God should not be an issue to anyone because everybody could be honest and loving enough to be such parts. In a metaphysical/real sense it will never be possible to identify who are parts of God, unless perhaps a political system can be formed whereby only honest loving people are allowed to administer the system. In such a case living honest loving people will each be a mere good bureaucrat who serves the public. Only the group as a whole will have the power to implement good policy for the whole.

Thoughts lead to the struggle between business and government. Businesses do not like taxation and bureaucracy. A source of the problem is printing of money, because those closest to the printing of money have best access to capital, to develop ideas. How can this be overcome to equalise society? The taxation problem can be overcome by printing money instead of taxing people and businesses, but much research will be needed to effectively replace taxation with printing of money. An idea is to regard shares of institutions as money. Such a system will put a mathematical brake on the printing of currency. Values of currencies will be determined by dividing value above the line by the number of shares/currency units, below the line. If money/shares are printed below the mathematical dividing line, without paying for the creation of value above the line, the value of currency units will depreciate. The value of currencies will in such a system not be primarily dependent on supply and demand, because institutions can be valued. The value of one unit of money/share, theoretically will be the value of the whole organisation divided by the number of units issued. There will be many currencies, which will be traded on something similar to current Stock Exchanges. Logically a reserve currency to value all other currencies will be needed. The reserve currency can be the currency of bureaucrats, which replaces taxation, and used to create order.

What will governments look like and how will they come into being? Members of Parliaments will each be independent in governments of national unity. Members will be appointed by voting. No overriding philosophy will be relevant like in communist, monarchial, democratic, oligarchic, theocratic or capitalist states. Party politics could be regarded as sectarianism, which divides nations. Only the two ideas Truth and Love will be above bureaucrats and they will be tested with *honery* testing, which they can have done voluntarily, if they want to be bureaucrats. That is, their honesty levels, in compliance with Truth; and actions in compliance with Love can be tested. Why should misleaders be in leadership positions? It does not make sense logically. Socrates's view that rulers must be allowed to lie to citizens is not acceptable. A problem is, how can *honery* tests be done? During previous research it became clear, part of society opines it is impossible. Logically it could be possible to simply explain to people what is meant by the ideas Truth and Love, and honest and loving behaviour. Then they can be simply asked whether they are honest and loving. If they are deceiving and non-loving the test should show it and then they become entrepreneurs, because they cannot be bureaucrats who have good ideas. The education system can teach children from a young age what is meant by the relevant words. Each person can decide whether they want to be an honest loving bureaucrat or an entrepreneur.

Another change from current democracies will be recognition of the role, nobles had in aristocratic historical governments. A synonym of the word noble is honest. Aristocracies make logical sense if they are really noble (honest), because good ruling, effectively, is partly a result of being honest and loving. Honest loving people have the best ideas because their minds are best equipped to have good ideas. The respect, nobles had for Truth, and the good creative effect that had during feudal systems, were rejected in democratic systems, partly because "nobles" were corrupted, before feudalism collapsed. The respect for Truth has to be reinstated with the respect for Love, added to the system. Bureaucrats should have respect for those two ideas and have financial security if they respect the two ideas. If it is claimed they did not respect the two ideas, they should be given a chance to defend themselves. Theoretically, the more honest and loving people are, the more financial security they should have. This can be ensured by *honery* tests, which can be voluntary. *Honery* testing is a rather cold idea for entrepreneurs and is probably a reason why a systematic attempt on the Internet was launched to change the meaning of the word *honery*. When I used the word *honery* for the first time, Google's search engine, did not pick up any results for the word. Since 2011 when I first used the word, the Internet has been flooded with definitions, names and probable back dating, which indicates opposition to the bureaucratic idea of *honery* testing.

With regard to other professions like the priesthood, medicine and engineering, tongue-in-cheek, they should all be divided between bureaucrats and entrepreneurs. The honest loving bureaucrats should work for states. Good entrepreneurs should develop the bureaucrats' good ideas, which bureaucrats can impart to the entrepreneurs without utilitarian stealing of ideas. Another possibility for an entrepreneur, to make a living, would be selling functional nonsense to the part of the public who cannot distinguish between truth and fallacy.

The ideas already mentioned here is starting to look like a proposal for a new type of state. I do not have enough experience to write a holistic view for a new form of state. No single human being has the knowledge to do that. I will just add lastly two opinions. I have some experience of the legal and auditing professions. My legal experience originated from a long Labour and Constitutional Court battle I had with UNISA since 2013 and a false charge of assault against me in the Magistrates Court at the same time. I defended myself against two men who attacked me at my home. No one needed medical help, but I was victimised for almost two years in the Magistrates Courts, from the same day I started a Labour Court case against UNISA. I realised the legal system does not work properly, because good rules, included in the Labour Act and Constitution were not applied. Examples of such rules are academic freedom and religious freedom and division between civil and criminal cases. Much evidence and recordings were tampered with and a lot of fraud took place during these cases. Poor people have almost no access to the legal system, therefore the legal system will work much better if honest loving legally qualified people work directly for the state and are paid by the state, in order to give all people the same rights and representation before the Law. With regard to the auditing profession: I never enjoyed doing public auditing work and I realised recently partly why that happened. The auditing system is irrational because although public auditors are supposed to police their clients, they are paid by their clients. All public auditors should be paid directly by the state.

This book does not have the purpose of proposing a new form of state. Much more studying would be needed for that, by many more people. The primary function is to promote the two ideas Truth and Love above bureaucrats, because, *intequity* is dependent on the acceptance of the two ideas, by as many people as possible. The idea *intequity* is important for sustainability of large populations. Hopefully eventually, a kind of reached balance, between population numbers and use of natural resources in a sustainable way, will be reached.

List of references

AQUINAS; T. 1273. *Summa theologica: treatise on the theological virtues: of the act of faith, article 4: whether it is necessary to believe those things which can be proved by natural reason?* From: http://www.sacred-texts.com/chr/aquinas/summa/sum257.htm on 19 June 2013.

BOTHA; M.E. 1988. *Objectivity under attack: rethinking paradigms in social theory – a survey.* In: Marshall, PA and Vander Vennen, R, eds. Social sciences in christian perspective, 33-62. Lanham, Md.: University Press of America.

BST. From: http://www.biblestudytools.com/lexicons/greek/kjv/chrestotes.html on 23 Sep 2017.

DESCARTES; R. 1641. *Meditations on First Philosophy.* In: Internet Encyclopedia of Philosophy, 1996; The Philosophical Works of Descartes, 1911. Cambridge University Press. From: http://selfpace.uconn.edu/class/percep/DescartesMeditations.pdf on 20 Sep 2017.

HOBBES; T. 1651. *Leviathan*, edited by C.B. Macpherson. London: Penguin Classics, 1985.

KEARNEY; R. 2011. *Anatheism: returning to God after God.* New York: Columbia University Press.

NIETZSCHE; F. 1886. *Beyond Good and Evil, Prelude to a Philosophy of the Future.* London: Penguin, 3rd edition, 2003.

NIETZSCHE; F. 1888. *The Antichrist.* In: Twilight of the Idols with The Antichrist and Ecce Homo. Ware, Hertfordshire: Wordsworth Classics, 2007.

PLATO. 350BC. Definitions. In: *Plato Complete Works*; edited by Cooper & Hutchinson. Cambridge: Hackett, Kindle edition, Location 46914, 1997.

PLATO. 350BCb. *The republic,* translated by Desmond Lee. London: Penguin, 2007.

ROBERTS; J.M. 1995. *The Penguin History of the World.* London: Penguin Group, 3rd edition.